When I Grow (Blow) Up

Pam Ryans, Author

.........When I Grow (Blow) Up

Pam Ryans, Author

Co-Author_____

Rian's Factory, Publisher

Parents:

"When I Blow (Grow) Up" is a goal-setting, interactive workbook. It helps children begin thinking about their future. I do realize that, as parents, you'll have many, many, "I want to be" conversations. This is just a start.

This book helps to introduce young minds to **colors, diversity, friends, imagination, numbers, prayer, and shapes.**

Once the child has completed all of the pages, they will be the Co-Author of "this" particular book. How exciting!!!

........When I Grow (Blow) Up

Rian's Factory Publishing, a Division of 1Vision Empowerment, LLC
Author Pam Ryans, Owner/Founder of 1 Vision Empowerment, LLC
(www.1visionempowerment.com)

ISBN-13: 978-0692396551
ISBN-10: 0692396551

Printed and Manufactured in the United States of America

FIRST PRINTING: March, 2015

When I Grow (Blow) Up

Pam Ryans, Author

Do you know what you want to be when you grow up? God does. Have you asked Him about it? This book helps begin a conversation with God about the future.

Jeremiah 29:11 says - "For I know the plans I have for you," declares the Lord, "plans to prosper you and not to harm you, plans to give you hope and a future." (NIV)

Matthews 7:7 says "Ask and it will be given to you; seek and you will find; knock and the door will be opened to you." (NIV)

Since, God has plans for you, then you should just ask Him.

DEDICATION

This book is dedicated to my grandson, LaRon and
my granddaughter, Amariya.

Granny loves you.

REMEMBER...

You can be anything with the love of Jesus!!

CHILDREN

This book is for you!!

Be sure to color all the pictures on each page.

And guess what then?

You will be the Co-Author of "THIS" Book!!!

Be sure to write your name on the blank line on this page and on the "Author" page, once you finish the entire book.

Co-Author _____

YOUR NAME

This is a conversation between shape friends in their classroom. They are talking about what they want to be when they grow up.

I hope you enjoy!

SHAPE FRIENDS

Square

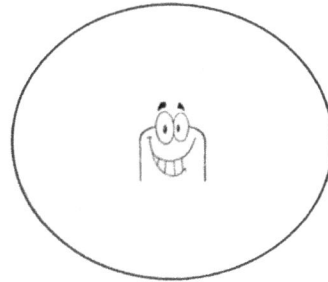

Circle

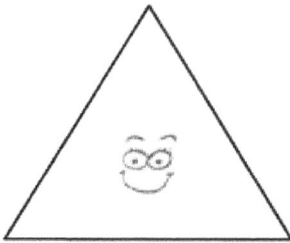

TRIANGLE

Star

Color chart for each shape in the book:

Color each Square, in the book, Green

Color each Circle, in the book, Blue

Color each Triangle, in the book, Red

Color each Star, in the book, Yellow

COLOR each crayon.

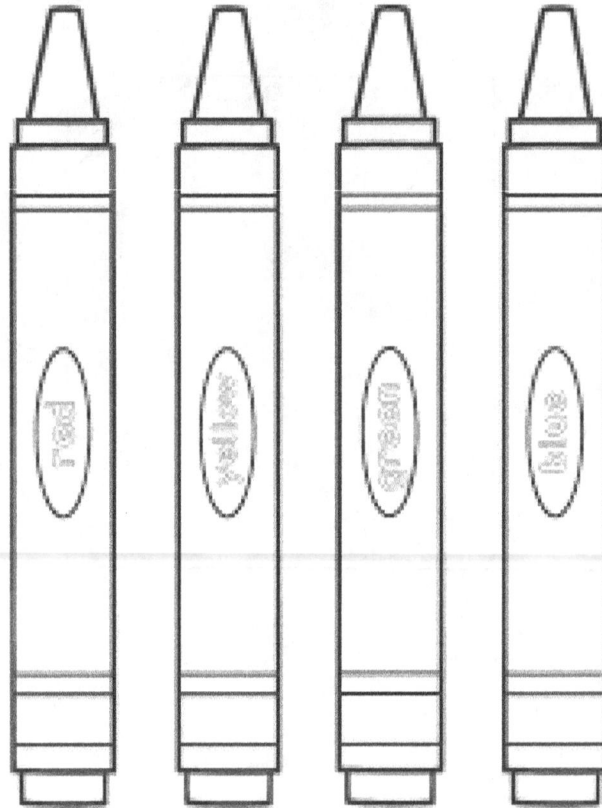

Green ☐ Square   Blue ◯ Circle

Red △ Triangle   Yellow ☆ Star

When you see this crayon poster, place a check ✓ mark in the box to show that you are finished with this page.

(Parent/Care-giver – this task will help the child's ability to be organized)

On a bright sunny day, four shape friends were in class.

What do you want to be when you grow up?

Square

Circle

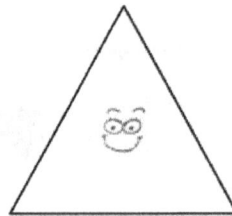
TRIANGLE

Star

What do you want to be when you grow up?

Square

Star

Square

So I can help people stand tall.

Square

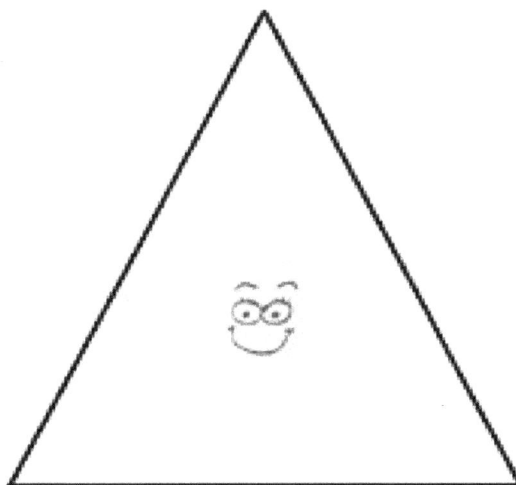

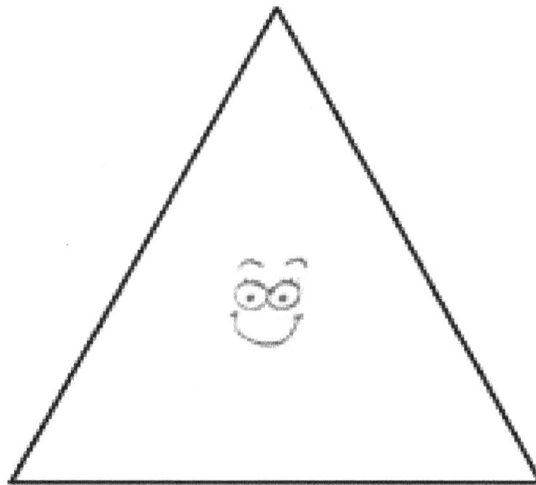

What about you, Circle?

Square

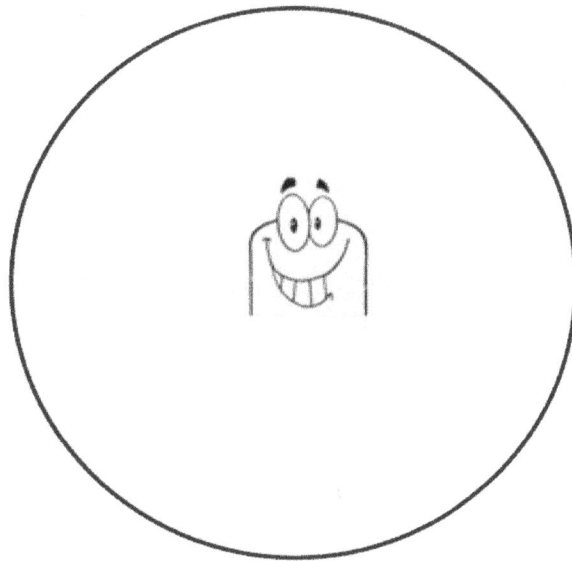

Circle

Circle, I can help you!

Star

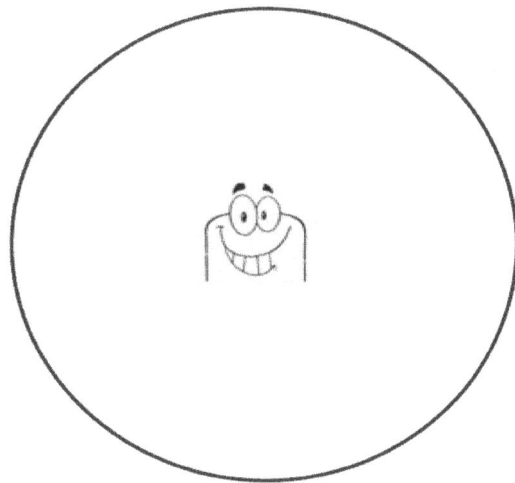

Circle

Tonight,
when you say your prayers,
ask God what you should be
when you grow up.

Star

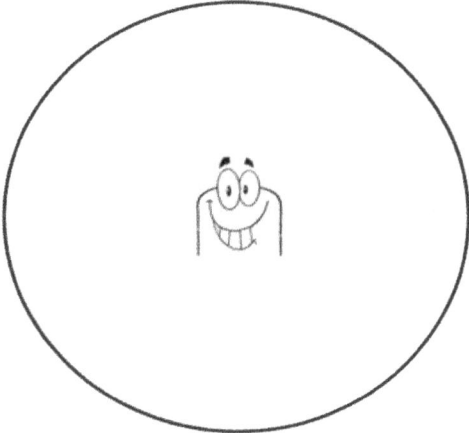

Later that night
Circle says his prayers before going to sleep.

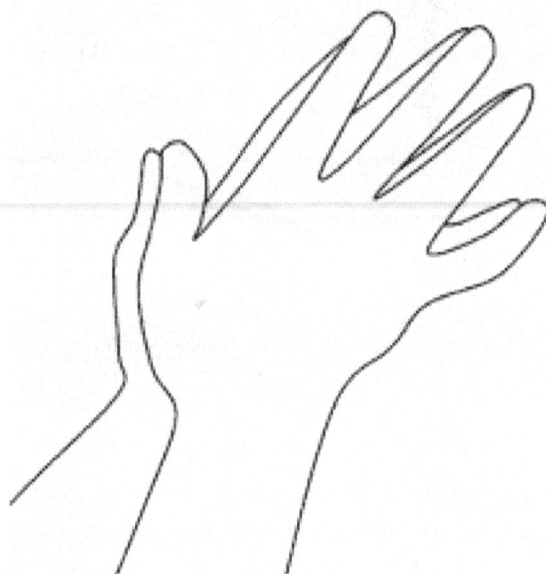

"God,
what do you want me to be?"

Circle

The next day at school.

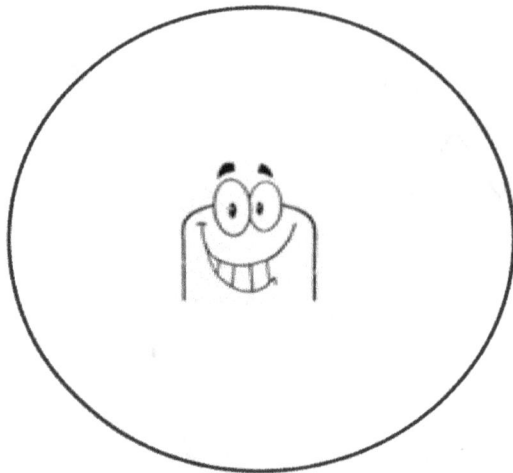

Circle

Circle

I can fly high in the sky.

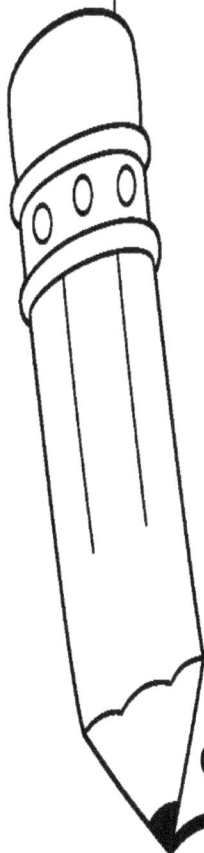

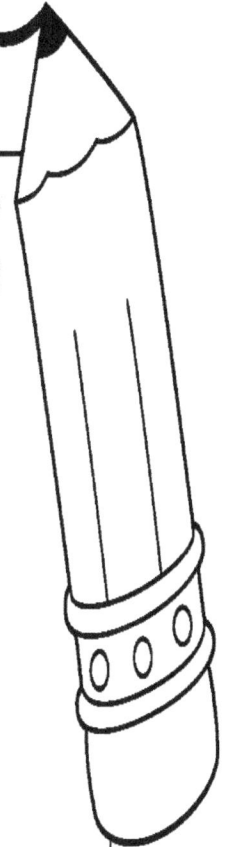

Color the Balloon in your favorite COLOR.

The End!!

Tonight, ask God what he wants YOU to be.

Now, go back to the front of the book and write your name on each blank line, as the Co-Author.

Thanks for your help.

Be blessed!!

I can fly high in the sky.

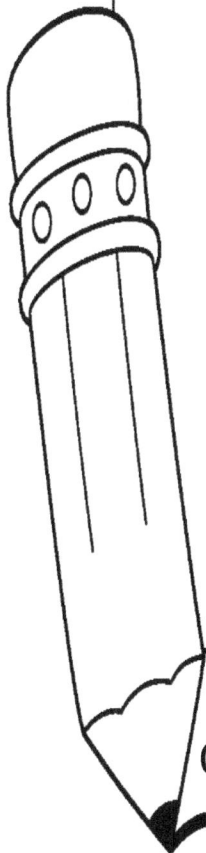

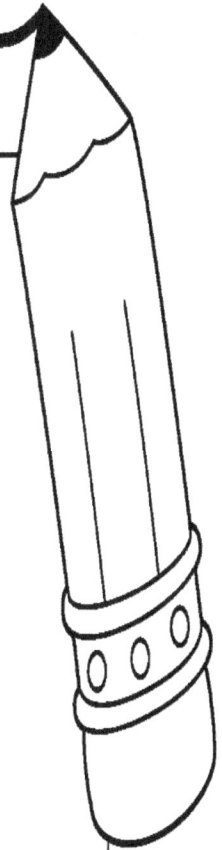

Color the Balloon in your favorite COLOR.

The End!!

Tonight, ask God what he wants YOU to be.

Now, go back to the front of the book and write your name on each blank line, as the Co-Author.

Thanks for your help.

Be blessed!!